# THE
# LAST OF THE
# WALLENDAS
### And Other Poems

# THE
# LAST OF THE
# WALLENDAS
## And Other Poems

### Russell Hoban

*illustrations by Patrick Benson*

*Hodder
Children's
Books*

a division of Hodder Headline plc

Edited by Vic Parker
Designed by Janet Watson

Published by Hodder Children's Books 1997

10 9 8 7 6 5 4 3 2 1

ISBN 0340 66766 4

Printed and bound in Great Britain by
MacKays of Chatham plc, Chatham, Kent

Hodder Children's Books
A division of Hodder Headline plc
338 Euston Road
London NW1 3BH

# Contents

*for Ben, Dan and Kobi*
*and*
*Elias, Ilana and Alisa*

# The Plughole Dragon

Down the plughole winking, blinking,
No one knows what he is thinking.
No one knows why he should be
living there so blinking free.

Did he swim there, did he crawl there?
Did he grow from very small there?
When the water's all run out,
why does he still hang about?

Dragon dimly, dragon darkly,
dragon down the plughole sparkly –
dragon, you with circled eyes,
if I call you, will you rise?

# 03.00 Abroad

Quietly, somewhere across the darkened town,
a clock struck three. It spoke
its hour in a friendly way, as if to say,
"Hello, I think we've met before." I
wasn't sure – the time seemed
different here, clothed in a distant
night and in a foreign place; I didn't
think I'd recognise its face until it
softly said, "Remember me?"
"Ah, yes," I said, "you're three."

# Crystal Maze

"Think about it," Harry said: "infinite regress."
That's my brother Harry; he knew how to give me
stress.
Coloured lights around us, music, laughter, shrieks
and yells,
the roar and clatter of the rides, the fun-fair with
its smells
of mustard and of frying;
there were pitchmen shouting, babies crying,
punters winning great pink teddy bears
and so on – it was pretty much like other fairs
I'd been to other summer days
except I'd never seen a Crystal Maze.

"It's just a hall of mirrors," Harry said –
"it's no big deal unless you lose your head.
You want to try it? Want to have a go?"
"I'm not so sure about this, Harry, I don't know.
What is it with this infinite regress?
Is that when more and more gets less and less?"
"Of course," he said, "it's only an illusion.
The thing you must avoid, though, is confusion:
there are angles and reflections
which can take you in directions
that could bring you to a place that I won't mention:

we're talking danger here, you
can't let them disappear you,
or you'll end up well into the fourth dimension."

We bought our tickets then,
and I sort of shivered when
I saw a hundred of us or a thousand, maybe more.
"Don't look at those," said Harry – "keep your eyes
down on the floor;
then you'll see what isn't mirror
and with luck we'll find the way
that will get us home today."

So I kept on looking down
though I felt my head go round
and the hundreds and the thousands of me
sometimes pulled me, sometimes shoved me
into strange and spooky places
where I saw all kinds of faces
that were not my brother Harry and they
certainly weren't me.

But finally I was out
and I gave a happy shout:
I said, "Harry, we have done it,
we have beat it, we have won – it
was a scary thing to do
but we have made it, me and you."
But Harry didn't answer because Harry
wasn't there.

Well, I told the man outside and we went in
and we tried
to find my brother Harry but we never found a
clue.
So he scratched his head awhile and he smiled
a sorry smile,
and he gave our money back – it was the best that
he could do.
When I came home all alone
I heard both my parents groan –
first my dad and then my mother
said, "You've come home short one brother,
which is more than somewhat careless, it's a
silly thing to do;
we think you'd best be grounded for a week or
maybe two."

And when I cleaned my teeth that night
the mirror gave me quite a fright –
the face I saw was not my face
but in another time and space
my brother Harry in the glass
looked out at me but could not pass
from that place I will not mention
homeward through the fourth dimension.

We change the mirror every week;
we've called in mediums to seek
my brother on whatever plane
he is, to bring him back again
but nothing helps. I've tried and tried
to cross him over to this side
but there he stays – though bright they shine,
I'm brushing Harry's teeth, not mine.

# Three Ducklings

## Crossing a Footpath

Ducklings are the shape of hurry.
Do they worry as they scurry
after Mum?

## Swimming

Behind each one its tiny wake
is all the waves that it can make.

# The Story Tree

In a country where I've been on holiday
there is a park: a fountain sends its spray
into the air above a pond where
ducks quack to each other; there
are statues, avenues of trees,
and I remember one of these:
a maple with a story of no words,
all sun and shadow, rustlings of birds,
its branches knobbed and twisting –
so many of them, each insisting
this was how the story went,
while others disagreed, and leant
towards new beginnings, wayward wendings,
odder plots with stranger endings.
The story changed to something else each day,
the wind and leaves all shadowing a different way
and always telling, telling, telling something new –
hard to believe sometimes but always true.
Sometimes I close my eyes and see that tree
and listen to the story that it whispers me.

# The Owl-Woman

"Do you love me?" says the owl-woman,
long legs reaching for the ground as she lands,
yellow eyes burning into mine.
Snowy white and speckled brown she is, from the
North she comes to my dreams and says,
"Do you love me?" always the same, from
the North, where the ice bear
swims in the sea, miles from the land, never lost.
"Yes," I say, "I love you."
"Do you think I am beautiful?" says the owl-woman,
sunlight through her wings, turning and turning,
yellow eyes burning. "Say it," she says.
"Yes," I say, "you are beautiful."
"I know," she says. "Now you can sleep."

# Pigeon on the Circle Line

Got on at Paddington and then
got off again at High Street Ken.
Maybe it found that flying was too hard;
maybe it had a Senior Pigeon Travelcard.

# Not My Day

I got up on the wrong side of the day
and came right off; it walked away
showing the whites of its eyes. "Stop!"
I said, "I mean to get on top
of you." It kept on going;
I followed, knowing
days don't always do
exactly what you'd like them to.
"Stand still," I said, "I'm going to try again."
I thought I heard it neigh a little, then
it kept on walking while I stood there talking.
"All right," I said (it sounded like a threat),
"I'll see you later." But I haven't yet.

# Room 18,
# National Gallery

I don't know if you've ever been
to see the peepshow that's in Room 18:
*Views of the Interior*, is how it's listed
*of a Dutch House*. Perhaps you've missed it?
It's well worth visiting; that's where
they've got a little dog who isn't there.
I mean (I'm trying not to cause confusion),
that little dog is an illusion
painted on wood by Samuel van Hoogstraten
(a name, I think, not soon to be forgotten),
but done so as to look 3-D:

peep through the peep-hole and you see
this little spotted dog sat in his place.
He has a somewhat melancholy face;
flat on the floor he's painted, partly up a wall.
He listens patiently to all
the things I say; he talks to me as well,
but what he says I mustn't tell.

# Lion Bells

Those four bronze lions in Trafalgar Square –
I'm not quite certain that they're always there.
They may be just exactly as they seem
but on the other hand, I had a dream
in which those lions all got up and left their post;
it was so real, really, much more so than most
dreams are. No roaring, all they did was ring
like big bronze bells, a most unusual thing.
And why, I wonder, did they leave their places?
One day I'll ask them to their faces.
I'll have to wait, of course, till some time when
they ring like big bronze bells again.

# The Dream of the Kraken

Vast in the circles of my
terror in the deep, agelong I weep,
shuddering, shivering, fearful of sleep,
dreaming the dream of myself that they keep
in the dark of the mind that they go there to find –
the dreamers who dream of
the Kraken.
I am so afraid! So afraid that
I am what they dream, that I am as I seem, as
agelong I weep, shuddering, shivering, cold
in the deep, dreaming the dream of
the Kraken.

# Kong

Fifty feet high, and like some awful dream –
when Fay Wray saw him she let out a scream
and so did I, almost: it was a monster fright,
and still that film brings back the old delight.
I do think, though, that they were wrong
in never making one whole giant Kong.
I didn't expect the real thing, for pity's sake,
but still, they could have made a full-scale fake;
it would have been the decent thing to do.
The full-size bits he had, they were so few!
A giant head of course; one giant hand;
one giant foot on which he couldn't stand.
A little jointed puppet climbed the Empire State
and mounted to the spire where Kong met his fate.
I've seen it many times; I won't forget
the way they shot him down – that's with me yet.
Bleeding from all his wounds and up so high
he knew by then that he was going to die;
he looked his last upon her face so sweet
and then he took that long fall to the street.
Kong's life was an illusion, yet I feel
he was somebody, and his death was real.

# Who Did Then?

With smoke and flame erupting from
the sea's dark deep, a hump arose with
lightnings and with thunder, under it
a being hooked of nose and chin, red-faced,
with painted eyes, and swazzle-shouting,
"ROOT-TOOT-TOO-IT!"
Clouds fled before it, women wept and babies
cursed; squadrons of angels dropped their
bright trumpets, scattered like starlings,
darkened the sky. "O God!" they sang *a capella*,
"Now you have done it!"
God only laughed and said,
"Oh no, I didn't."

# Monsters

Why is it that I always find
monsters living in my mind,
monsters lurking in my books,
giving me such dirty looks?
    I wonder about that sometimes.

You do not need to be eighteen
to read of monsters really keen
on naked ladies chained to rocks –
just one of many monster shocks.
    OK, it provides employment for heroes.

I'm fond of horror films, but slime
is dripping faster all the time
from ugly things with many teeth
and other ugly things beneath.
    Not too many clean-cut monsters about.

The old-time monsters that I view
are much more cosy than the new:
the creature from the black lagoon,
I won't forget him very soon;
he couldn't seem to get it right
but basically he was polite.
And Kong – it would have made his day
to get a kind word from Fay Wray.
Poor Kong – so sad to see him fall!
I think I like him best of all.
  They don't make monsters like they used to.

# Ice Bears

"Polar bears face extinction and a large number of
other animals will be reduced to tiny remnant
populations by global warming in the Arctic regions,
the World Wide Fund says in a report today."

News story by Paul Brown,
*The Guardian*, 17 December 1996

Huge, silent-moving like
white dreams hungering for
the yester-prey,
what will they do when
the ice is gone?

Will they move south, wear
brightly-coloured sports shirts,
drink Coca-Cola?

Will they sleep in
cardboard boxes, beg for
small change?

Or will they, knowing how
things end, swim on
and on and on
into the darkness,
when the ice is gone?

# The Last of the Wallendas

*13 May 1996*

Reading the paper and shaking his head,
my father looked thoughtful. "What is it?" I said.
"It's Helen Wallenda," he told me. "She's dead –
the last of them all, and she died in her bed."
"Who were the Wallendas?" I wanted to know.
"How well I remember," he said, "when we'd go
to the circus and see them way up there so high,
and no net below them – at least that's how I
see it now in my mind, all the glitter and gleam
of the dazzling Wallendas, the high-wire team:
those silvery bicycles moving so slow,
with the music all breathless and Death down
below,
and the balance poles wavering, catching the light
as the fearless Wallendas crossed high in the night,
with Karl in a chair perching up at the top
and nothing below but a forty-foot drop.

All gone now – some early and some of them late,
they came off the wire and met their high fate.
Her husband, old Karl, the greatest of all,
was ten storeys up when the wind made him fall.
So brave and so daring and all of them dead!
But Helen Wallenda, she died in her bed."

# Foggy Morning

This foggy morning, after the rain,
Oliver Mole lies newly slain –
big hands empty, velvet coat unsleek.

Emily Cat, contented soul,
laps up milk from her little blue bowl,
purring loud and meek.

Late last night, with the raindrops drumming,
Oliver didn't hear death coming:
caught in the dark at his tunnel's door,
Oliver digs our lawn no more.

Peaceful, purring Emily Cat
washes her face on the back-door mat.

# Turtle Prince?

Jim Frog sat on a lily pad;
he was feeling lonesome, feeling sad,
feeling more than somewhat fed-up
when a snapping-turtle stuck her head up
(caused a few ripples round the pond),
said, "Hello, sailor! Do not despond!
I fancy you, and I'll be quite frank –
although I'm of superior rank
(I'm a turtle princess, actually),
I'm asking you to marry me.
This offer is too good to miss;
now, how about a great big kiss?"

Jim knew the stories; he'd read the books.
He didn't really like her looks;
her forthright manner made him wince,
but still, he thought – a turtle prince!
So he kissed her. I haven't seen him since.

# Long-Gone Pearl

Johannes Vermeer (1632-1675)
*Girl with a Pearl Earring*

(Postcard from the The Hague)

I call her Pearl; her face on a card
is asking a question; I find it hard
to know what it is she's trying to say
as she looks at me in her wistful way.
Her eyes are sad, she never smiles;
in her pensive look is the sound of viols –

Golden the voices, yearning slow,
speaking of Pearl with string and bow,
viols agleam in the candle's light,
seeking her face in the long, long night.

Her lips shape a word that's still unspoken
and her printed silence remains unbroken.
Speak to me, do, dear postcard girl –
what are you thinking, long-gone Pearl?

# Alison Vickers

Alison Vickers has many a time
wished that her name were less easy to rhyme –
I mean, really!

One day at the beach with a party from school
she was hit by a wave and she felt such a fool
when it drew back and left lower Alison bare,
exposed to all eyes and the balmy salt air
in her teeny-weeny bikini top.

Now all of the boys smile at Alison Vickers,
remembering that time when the sea took her
dignity away.

# *Mermaid*

Mermaid, mermaid,
green-glimmering in the deeps,
pearly-naked gliding
where the Kraken sleeps!
Ancient is the ocean of my mind;
in its full-moon waters
you I find,
mermaid!

# Big Stone Women
# of Vienna

Big stone women don't get tired –
that's why they're hired
to hold up buildings in so many different places.
With their beautiful sad faces
full of patient resignation
and acceptance of their station,
shouldering theatres, shops, and banks,
and never a word of thanks
though there's no place in this town
where they've let a building down.
Take a good look all around:
they've not let one building down!

For those noble big stone beauties,
always faithful to their duties,
all together, let us hear
one tremendous rousing cheer,
for they never caryatidn't and they always caryatid
as they jolly well were bid.

Hip, hip, hooray! Two more, I say!
Hip, hip, hooray! Hip, hip, hooray!
Big stone women of Vienna!

# Long Green Dream

Last night there came a long green dream,
it pulled in like a train.
I climbed aboard and found a seat, it started
off again
and chuntered on and on and on to oh, so
many places
with place-names that I couldn't read and
hundreds of strange faces.
We journeyed half-again as long as any trip
should take,
and yet it got me back on time, and brought
me to Awake.

# The Raiders

I'm thinking of a road that climbed a hill.
We were quite high; the summer air was still;
below us crows were soaring; under them a farm
sat snugly in a valley – safe from harm
it seemed, but all around me I could feel the eyes
of long-dead raiders bent upon a prize;
could hear, almost, the hiss of bright blades drawn.
I blinked; back into silence they were gone;
the ancient past had swallowed up its dead
and left me thoughtful, watching in their stead.

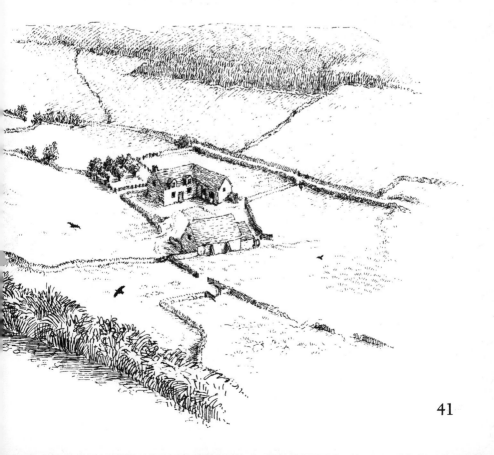

# Long, Lone

Long, long, long and lone
is the selkie's song when the storm winds moan,
is the sigh of the sea as it rubs the stone,
is the word of the sea that lives in the bone.

Long and lone is the gliding flight
of the albatross in the dawn's grey light
on its wide white wings where the winds blow high
over the waves where the sea-ghosts cry.

Long and lone is the sea I find
that sighs on the shore at the edge of my mind;
long, long, long and lone
is the word of the sea that lives in the bone.

# What the Crow Knows

There is this crow, I see him on the common
every day –
he has a certain walk that seems to say,
"I know a thing that you don't know."
I've said to him, "Please tell me, Mr Crow,
what is this thing that you know that I don't?"
I do think he could tell me but he won't;
he nods his head and shakes his wings and walks
that certain way but never, never talks.

# Rodney's All Right Now

"Thousands of bears are kept in conditions like these on
farms in China and milked of the bile from the gall bladder,
sold as a traditional cure."

From a news story by Daniel McGrory,
The Times, 18 December 1996

Ursa Major, up in the sky
and Ursa Minor, they'll never die.
Safe forever among the stars –
Great Bear and Little Bear, no iron bars.
 (My teddy bear, Rodney, now he's blind,
 he says he's got more peace of mind.)

Chinese civilisation is a wonderful thing;
think of gunpowder, acupuncture, the I Ching.
The Great Wall stretches for mile after mile
and they bury their emperors in imperial style.
 (My teddy bear, Rodney, he said today,
 "I don't want to see this – take it away.")

A bear lies clamped in a filthy cage,
moaning in pain and crazed with rage;
a tube in its gall bladder drains off bile
and steel straps keep it from moving the while.
The photo was in this morning's *Times*;
right in the "Home News", not with "Crimes".
   (Rodney didn't know what to do –
   he couldn't stand the sight;
   I took out both his button eyes and
   now he's quite all right.)

# The Dragon Klong

The dragon Klong, he has a bag in
which he carries lots of dragon
bonbons, sweets, and munchies –
all kinds of things he likes to chew,
like nuts and bolts, perhaps a few
old rusty pipes and crunchies.
He's very fond of iron frogs,
he catches them in iron bogs
or underneath the sink.
Each iron frog weighs half a stone –
they make Klong belch, they make him groan,
they also make Klong klink.

# The Green Bronze
# Lady by the
# Albert Bridge

The green bronze lady of F. Derwent Wood, R.A.,
in green bronze thought she passes night and day.
Modestly naked, with a touching grace,
she looks on time with the specific face
of some remembered girl – she's not
a nymph or goddess that can be forgot.
Born 1871, died 1926,
F. Derwent Wood in bronze her beauty fixed.

# Thames Full Moon

That's it – those
broken silver glimmers, all those
scatterings of brightness, rocking
silver ripples, broken-circled, holding
one round silvery idea of moon.
In fragmented and water-shivered
glimmers all down Chelsea Reach the river
keeps on thinking, moon, moon,
moon – a moon is in the
river there below you anywhere you stand. Tell me,
how many are there? You go to that lamp,
I'll take this one. Now I see a
moon below me; so do you. I'll move to
the next lamppost. Still there is a

moon to look at in the water just below me. Go on
to the farthest lamppost down the reach –
a moon is in the water there by each.
Why is that? Don't say an answer from a book;
look. One moon in the sky; how many in the river?
I don't want an answer from a book.
Look.

# Portknockie

The sky was darkening, though golden light was still
on Green Castle, Bow Fiddle, Port Hill.
The tide was up, the pebbles rattled on the strand;
the evening breeze was blowing from the land
towards where a cormorant beat its way above the
dazzle of the sea.
The old man sighed a little, then he said to me,
"I think of the old days, the shouts and the noise
and the boats coming in with the men and the boys
and the women all laughing, the girls and the wives –
and then it was over, that part of our lives,
when the herring stopped coming."

"But why did they stop?"
I asked him. He shrugged. "They just closed up the shop,
they put up the shutters and all went away,
and the cause of it nobody knows to this day."

I tried to imagine the shouts and the noise
and the boats coming in with the men and the boys
and the brown sails well filled with the winds of
the past,
but all I could hear was the silence at last
as I looked at the photos the old man showed me
and the harbour held out empty arms to the sea.

# TV Horror

By full moon, also when the moon is new,
in oakwood forest or beneath the yew
some loathsome lurking monster softly stalks
the poor benighted traveller who walks
in fear and trembling, never looking back
to see the thing that follows on his track.
With baited breath we hear a mournful cry:
the owl's dark warning that a death is nigh.

I really do not want to be a bore,
but here's a thing I notice more and more:
whether the scene is Cheshire, Somerset, or Kent,
those TV owls hoot with the same accent.
Why do so many sound the same?
I know there's some executive to blame.
If actors learn to speak both posh and yokel,
why can't those ruddy local owls hoot local?
I've written letters and I promise to applaud
if ever I should hear a Yorkshire owl hoot broad.

# Chopin – Mazurka in A Minor, Opus 67, No. 4

Love and death and sweet romance –
come and see the shadows dance!
See them circle, soft and slow;
see the faces come and go.
Slant the present to the past
while the notes, remembering, last,
glimmering golden candlelight
on keys of black, keys of white:
love and death and sweet romance –
come and see the shadows dance!

# The Ghost Horse of Chingis Khan

Chingis, Chingis, Chingis Khan,
galloping, galloping, galloping –
Chingis, Chingis, Chingis Khan,
where is the hill he lies upon?
Nobody knows.

Under what lost and lonely star,
galloping, galloping, galloping far,
galloping where the ghost herds are?
Nobody knows.

Thousands of horses now are one,
galloping, galloping, galloping.
Call with a whistle made of bone,
call up the bay, the grey, the roan,
ee-lu-lu-ee-ya-ee, now come,
come to my whistle, come to my drum,
come with the ghost of Chingis Khan,
strong on the herds he rode upon –
thousands of horses now are one,
ee-lu-lu-ee-ya-ee!

Under the moon, under the sun,
thousands of horses now are one;
thousands of days are one long night –
look with the dark, look with the bright,
look for the ghost of Chingis Khan,
strong on the horse he rode upon –
ee-lu-lu-ee-ya-ee!

Red is the ghost horse, red like flame,
bright in the darkness – speak its name,
keen as the bend of the Tartar bow,
galloping, galloping. Who can know
the name of the horse he rides upon?
Chingis, Chingis, Chingis Khan!

# Fred to Samantha

I've read somewhere: on Chesil Beach,
the sea sorts pebbles, each from each,
from large to small,
and smooths them all
with grinding, rubbing, rolling, rounding,
in the clicking tidewash sounding
under the gull's cry
and the long, lone sigh
of the wind.

I wondered, in my thoughts of you,
just how the two of us might do:
though I am short and you are tall
I hoped you would return my call;
I hoped the telephone would ring
to make my heart triumphant sing.
I hoped, in every wind and weather
the two of us might rub together.

But no, long silence fills the day
and all my hopes have ebbed away.
I think perhaps some colder sea
sorts me from you and you from me.

# The Death of Sergei Preminin

Summarised from "Seconds from Armageddon"
by Bob Flynn, *The Guardian*, 22 November 1996

On 3 October 1986, twenty-year-old Apprentice Seaman
Sergei Preminin*, having carried to safety an unconscious
colleague, went back into the gas-filled reactor chamber
of the Russian nuclear submarine K219 to stop a chain
reaction and prevent the meltdown that could have
triggered the launch of the sub's missiles. With his oxygen
almost gone, he cranked down the last reactor rod
manually. By the time he finished, the gas pressure had
sealed the escape hatch shut, he had no more oxygen,
and he died.

The K219 was three hundred miles off Bermuda at the
time, its sixteen missiles targeting Washington, New York,
and Boston. Disabled by a collision with the American
submarine shadowing it, the K219 had surfaced with an
open missile hatch and put the US on a DEFCON 2 alert
which would have led to war if the Russian missiles had
been launched.

Sergei Preminin was posthumously awarded the Red Star.

• • •

*pronounced *Prehmeen-yin*

# K219

Down three thousand fathoms deep,
deaths of millions in her keep;
with her, in eternal sleep,
Sergei Preminin.

Remembering a French film, I see,
from another time, a man in black with
a white ruff, bowing by candlelight a
burnished viol. "Tomb of Sorrows" he
plays, and his beautiful dead wife
appears to him and smiles.

Breathing and sighing, langorous and low,
the viol mourns, lamenting slow
the well-beloved who must go
back to the shadows.

What did they think, those in
the war rooms where they watched
on screens the bombers and the
battleships of nations? What were
the images, what was the music
in their minds?

> All centuries to the dead are one
> with that long time before time was begun –
> when comes that day when all our days are done,
> we join the company arrived before.
>
> That man long dead who played the viol,
> his dead wife with her tender smile –
> they'll spend eternity a while
> with Sergei Preminin.

# Miss Presser in Sloane Square

The way the fountain lady does her hair
(I mean the naked bronze one in Sloane Square) –
our new French teacher does it just the same:
a classic style. Miss Presser is her name.
That naked lady's so much like Miss Presser,
I find that mentally I have to dress her.

# Circles of Storks

Very, very, very high
in a clean and washed-out pale blue sky:
circles of storks overlapping, soaring, drifting,
wings outspread to catch the lifting
of the thermals rising from the valley.

This was in Israel, where the sky
is not what you and I
are used to here in London, no, it's
higher, deeper, wider;
very far it goes, and full of light –
well, it's a proper sky for God to write
circles of storks in.

# At Dimla

At Dimla when the moon was new
the streets were dark, their hopes were few.

At Dimla when they beat the drum
they hoped that nothing bad would come.

At Dimla when they sang the song
they tried to sing it not too long.

At Dimla when they barred the gate
they found they'd left it much too late
at Dimla.

# Dragon Into Dressing Gown

I know a dragon dark and green
(he's quite the handsomest I've seen)
who, sometimes less and sometimes more,
lives just behind my bedroom door.

And, sometimes less but often more,
that dragon just behind the door
rolls one eye up and one eye down
and turns into my dressing gown.

He doesn't do it in the night,
but in the early morning light
where dragon was, there on its hook
that dressing gown gives me a look.

I've asked the dragon if he'd stay
and be a dragon through the day,
but with a smile and with a frown
he turns into my dressing gown.

# It's Always Kee-wick

Two owls – what are they? Husband and wife?
Sister and brother?
One to the left, one to the right –
you'd think by now they'd recognise each other
across the common in the night,
but no, the farther one says, "Who?" and waits
to hear a name;
the nearer owl says, "Kee-wick!" every time
the same.
Sometimes, when the first one speaks its word
I make believe that I'm the second bird:
I say, "It's Harry, Bill, or Ken!"
But both owls know it's Kee-wick yet again.

# The Hippogriff

Long centuries have I soared above the Earth;
the mind of Ariosto gave me birth.
Sired by a griffon (he imagined) on a mare,
I course the currents of the upper air
(in his time unpolluted, crystalline, and pure
but now a mixture that I scarce endure
to breathe). My mighty pinions have grown tired;
I fly, no more by winged words inspired,
from habit only. What else can I do?
The times are out of joint, and heroes few.

No more do maidens chained to rocks
want rescue – now in tiny frocks
they seek out monsters more to be abhorred
than poor old Orca; all he hoped to do was eat
a juicy virgin for a little treat:
Angelica it was, Miss World of her time –
a real stunner; horrid was the crime
of sacrificing one so young in all her beauty,
but heroes then were sworn to do their duty;
and so Ruggiero sped to the attack
in heavy armour, mounted on my back.
I bore him swiftly to the fray;
he did the job and then we came away,
Angelica now riding in the pillion seat,
Ruggiero looking forward to his treat.
My youth is gone and shrivelled is my fame;
I'll end my days in some computer game
with characters whose lips move when they read
their circuits, myrmidons who need
no seas nor mountains, neither skies of blue.
How are the mighty fallen! My last hope is you.

# Sheepy-Time Goats

Sometimes, when I'm counting sheep,
trying hard to fall asleep,
goats are what I get instead,
jumping hurdles in my head.
"No use counting us," they say.
"Here we are and here we stay –
we're the thoughts you'd rather not
think but we have not forgot
anything. No, we have not
any little thing forgot.
Baa-aa-aa and hi-de-ho!
How you wish we'd jump and go
but we won't, and through your mind
we will hurdle till you find
all those times you'd rather not
think of but they're not forgot.
Stay awake and take it slow –
when we're done we'll let you
know."
Goats are just as good as sheep –
while they jump I fall asleep.

# Rivers In Your Mind

Those rivers that you meet on holiday –
you get to know them, then you go away.
But through the meadows and the pastures of
your mind,
in their meanders slowly do they wind,
each with its bit of sky, wind riffles or a
spattering of rain,
each with its views that go and come again:
those friendly rivers that you leave behind
go winding through the meadows of your mind.

# What the Fairy Said to the Bibliophile

The elderly hero of Anatole France's *The Crime of Sylvestre Bonnard* encounters, in a country library late one night, a beautiful fairy sitting on an old German leather-bound *Cosmography of Munster*.

• • •

He wasn't sure that he was seeing right:
there, sat before him in the candle's light,
a fairy woman with a queenly smile.
Her many charms were such as did beguile
that old man, made him feel quite young again,
made him uncertain where he was or when.
Her figure pleased him and her hair was blonde;
she held, quite properly, a hazel wand.
The time was well past midnight, I should think;
it might be that he'd had too much to drink –
at all events, he found it nothing shocking
to glimpse a shapely leg in a pink stocking:
gold-clocked it was, the height of Paris style;
perhaps there was flirtation in her smile?

A handsome woman, although very little –
her wit was quick, her patience somewhat brittle.
Was she, he wondered, really there?
To this she answered with a haughty air:
"Nothing is real," she said, (and here's the twist)
"except what is imagined; therefore I exist."
Or words to that effect. Now neurologic
experts find,
what the eye sees is mainly in the mind.
Anatole France knew this some time ago
and I as well confirm that it is so:
I know she really is imaginary –
that's why she's real, that chic pink-stockinged
fairy.

# The Dragon
# Underneath the Mat

The dragon underneath the mat,
he wore a shiny opera hat.
I always squashed it very flat
each time I trod upon the mat.

The dragon said that would not do,
the dragon said his wants were few:
a little peace; a little mat;
and no one flattening his hat.

I never thought how he might feel,
I trod him underneath my heel.
Yes, every day beneath that mat
his hat was squashed completely flat.

One day I found a little note
and this is what the dragon wrote:
"Goodbye, I'm leaving home. My hat
too often has been trodden flat."

I know that I was very wrong;
I think about it all day long;
I wish the hat had been more strong.
Sometimes I hum a dragon song.

# The Fighting Temeraire

"THESE BIRDS MUST BE KILLED"
                    Headline in the *Angling Times*, 4 December 1996

I saw a cormorant the other day,
sat on a rock; around him lay
dead anglers – there were nine or ten.
"What's this?" I said. "I'm culling fishermen,"
the bird replied. "I'd thought the sea
was big enough for them as well as me
but no, it seems to be their wish
that I shan't be allowed a single fish.
It's not as if they're likely to go short
at mealtime – they just kill for sport.
And so, if that's the way it's going to be,
from this day on it's either them or me."
And while I stood there pondering what to say,
the cormorant shook his head and flew away.

# Statuesque Modesty

There was this statue in the park – a woman
with no clothes on, smiling.
"Don't you feel ill-at-ease?" I said,
"naked among the trees?"
"Not at all," she said. "No question here of crudity –
I am completely covered by my nudity."
"But tell me," I said, "have you ever had
a dream in which you find yourself
out in the street with all your clothes on?"
"Allow me, please," she said, "to put you in your
place:
if such a dream approached me I would slap
its face."

# The District Line at Notting Hill Gate

Sometimes early, sometimes late,
I get the District Line at Notting Hill Gate:
westbound is the platform where I wait.
That station's like a hangar where
the farther end is open to the air;
a bit of sky leans down into the cut.
Something about that place, I don't know what,
makes me feel long ago and far away,
remembering moments gone and words I didn't say.
Eight arches are the facing of a high brick wall –
it has a sixteenth-century look, and all
those arches lead me somewhere that I've
never been;
they take me to a place I've never seen,
this autumn evening, not too late:
the westbound platform, Notting Hill Gate.

# The Rendezvous at Zarmni

The dark ones came and the ones from the sea,
the mountain ones and the great unshapens:
all came to
Zarmni with the spring tides in the dark of the
moon. All came to Zarmni in the dark of the moon.

The ones who knew one word, the ones who knew
two and three, the ones with a sign or a gesture or
wearing a sigil, the ones who wept for the grass, sang
for the bone, scanned all the line of the
long, long ebbtide, walking like birds, birding their
thoughts of the sea at Zarmni.

And the ruins! The wind, how it sang on the stones,
sighed on the rubble, drummed on the wrecks that lay
stranded where the birds ran incessantly crying on the
tideline while other birds rose continually on the
rising air, continually spreading the slanting circles of
their thought, themselves the thoughts of the
wind that
blurred the lights of the coast, lights at sea,
seen lights and unseen at Zarmni.

And the dogs on the strand, the dogs like shadows, like
darkness that runs on four legs, the dogs
running silent between long rows of dead lamps on
the broken esplanade at Zarmni.
Strange oracles, strange timepieces, stone flutes,
bone whistles, drums in the smoke and the light of the
watchfires, and the auguries were good; all read the
auguries and they were good at Zarmni.
The auguries were good. And yet
when it came from the sea, when it parted the
fathomless waters, parted the air above them, darkened
the stars, swallowed the silence and did what it
did at Zarmni, no one was surprised.

# My Last Dragon

Forlorn he sits, and still forlorner,
alone and sad in his dark corner.
I said I'd write, I said I'd phone
but still he sits there all alone;
no one knows where to find him.

His scales are dull, his eyes are dim,
no fiery breath comes out of him;
all silent is his echoing roar,
his wings bear him aloft no more –
his battles are behind him.

I left him when at childhood's end
I waved to him as round the bend
of time he grew quite small, so small
that soon he wasn't there at all
except in memory.